The Birth of An Advocate

The Birth of An Advocate:

How My Son Helped Me Find My Voice

LaTanya S. Sothern

Pastor Mama Sheretta, Continue to make the hearts of people sparkle! Be the voice!

LaTanya S. Sothern

ISBN: 978-0-692-53587-5

This book is dedicated to my family and friends who have supported my beautiful struggle as a mother:

To Datosha who encouraged me when everything in me wanted to stop;

To my editors Sharon Foster and Joy Jackson - thanks for allowing me to trust you with my vision;

To my Pastors Drs. Mike and Dee Dee Freeman for providing the nest and nourishment for my spiritual development;

To my Dad Lamont Smith and my loving, late Grandparents for being my cheerleaders;

To the late Cathy Fox who became our biggest and greatest medical advocate before we knew how to do it on our own, who pushed Tré's little body towards health and who loved him unconditionally;

To my Mom Jean Smith, the one who taught me to advocate and is my best example of motherhood;

To my husband Greg, who graciously chose me as his crown. May I continue to shine for you every day;

To my youngest son, Quinton, who brings sparkly light and laughter into my life;

And to Tré, the one who helped me realize who I was inside and to tap into the strength that I didn't know I had. You have taught me so much more than I will ever be able to teach you. Mommy loves you bunches!

Prologue

Advocate: <u>**ad·vo·cate**</u> (noun) \ ˈad-və-kət, -ˌkāt \
1: One who pleads the cause of another; specifically one that pleads the cause of another before a tribunal or judicial court. 2: One that defends or maintains a cause or proposal. 3: One who supports or promotes the interests of another.

I chose to look up the definition of the noun "advocate" in order to get some background on the word itself, and dig into its original usage. It is a combination of the Latin "ad" (to) and "vocare" (call or voice). It literally means "to voice" or in my translation, "to be a voice": for someone, something, some cause. The verb "advocate" is defined as an active, not passive verb. You cannot be an advocate and let things happen around you -- not questioning, not speaking up. It is a performance, not an observation. An advocate is not a spectator; rather, an advocate is a participant. That's what I am, I am a voice, THE voice for my child. What an unlikely role for someone like me!

I was not much of a fighter as a child. In fact, growing up in the southeast quadrant of Washington, DC, (historically seen as having the lowest per-capita income of the four quadrants of the city), I stood out like a sore thumb. I was really tall for my age, and although I played outside and enjoyed my friends, I could be just as happy staying inside reading a book. I have described myself as "un-athletic," and was always one of the last picked to play on ANY team in P.E. I was quite timid, and as an only child, easily influenced by "alpha" personalities. I was, in my eyes at the time, a "punk" – easily defeated, cried at the drop of a hat, always wanted to please other people. I had difficulty finding a voice for myself. I would have been the last person to be found speaking for someone else.

Looking back, I could point to an unplanned coalition between my mother, my maternal grandmother, and a number of teachers and mentors who helped me develop into the person I became: popular, charismatic, self-confident, not afraid to speak up for myself when the time was appropriate. They all made sure I was a part of activities that developed my leadership skills: essay and poetry contests, community youth leadership organizations, church leadership activities, etc. High school meant more opportunities to develop skills that seemed to awaken as I grew older. The honor of giving my high school's valedictory address and a full college scholarship to American University as a Communications major served to propel me further into opportunities and avenues where my thoughts and opinions were not only welcomed, but also solicited and praised.

However, no one could have ever told me that I would give birth to a child whose success or failure in life would depend on my ability to advocate on his behalf, spiritually, medically, and academically. Me? No, you have the wrong one.

I'm the "crybaby" remember? I'm the one my family said was "tender-hearted" (like my maternal grandmother). I am the shrinking violet in times of adversity. I'm the "bookworm," the "smart-girl," not like the brash, sassy girls I saw and grew up with – girls who were not afraid to speak their minds, and would give you an earful at any given point in time if you looked at them the wrong way. I would have told you that you are mistaken, that can't be me, I'm too "this," too "that" or too "the other" to be **that** person. I would feel instant pity for that baby because I would have felt helplessly unequipped and unable to care for such a tiny, fragile creature with so many needs.

But indeed, I was (and am) that person; his voice, his champion, his applauder, his cheerleader, his booster, and his tub-thumper. And I have heard someone say that, "God doesn't call the equipped, He equips the called." He knew what I would be facing as an adult, and made sure that I had everything I needed to be able to meet this beautiful struggle of mothering and caring for my exceptional child. My life's journey brought me to this point, and looking back on my path, I now see how everything that I have done thus far has helped me with this most important work of being his mother. Looking back also gives me the confidence to know that everything I will need in the future to continue to be a loving wife to my husband, and an awesome mother to both of my children will be available for me, just as it was before. My job is not to know the "how," but rather to step out on faith towards the vision, and the how will happen as I move towards it.

Today, I wear the mantle of advocate for my children with pride, like a cape flapping in the wind, with a big shiny "A" on my chest! Yes I am "the advocate;" who else would it be? Who else will speak for them? Who else will navigate the system for them? Who else will be the voice? That's my God-given responsibility as a parent. This of course does not mean being a bully, rude or disorderly. Professional and polite has always been my manner, and I know that more people will hear my voice if it is seasoned with reason and logic. But that "punk" that I thought I was is long gone, and I will not allow people to escape their responsibilities and doing their jobs when it comes to getting the best for my children. And I am now trying to encourage other parents to do the same.

Furthermore, this role of advocate is also a spiritual one. Advocates pray for, build up and confess the Word of God over those in their care. They go to God as an intercessor for their loved ones. Sometimes, my role as a spiritual advocate is the only thing that's left to do when all other options or solutions seem to have been exhausted. It may not seem like it, but the role of advocate in the spiritual arena is even more important than it is in the natural arena.

So this is not just a book for parents of special needs children. It is for anyone who questions their role in speaking up for themselves, someone they are caring for, or something they care passionately about. It is your job to question, to push, and sometimes prod people into seeing that is in their best interests to fulfill their responsibilities – to use their sphere of influence to provide the best care for those you love. It is for any parent, or person in general, who needs encouragement and a reminder to know that there is a purpose for everything you are dealing with in your life right now. Your job is to extract the life lessons and meaning behind it all and use that information to guide and direct you into your destiny. Yes, life may have dealt you a tremendous blow, and you think it is too difficult to overcome, but as my Pastor, Mike Freeman, says, "If it is in your life, you can handle it."

You have been called; therefore you have been equipped.

Chapter One

A New Beginning

irst, I would have never imagined I would be here. As a little girl, I imagined myself as a single parent, happily raising my daughter alone. Being the child of a divorced single parent, marriage just wasn't on my radar – I mean, my mom was doing the single-parent thing, and doing it well in my eyes. Growing up in southeast DC, there weren't many examples of anything to the contrary.

Fast forward 25 plus years: now I find myself, a married woman, getting ready to give birth to a son, a man-child who would be named for my husband and his father before him. In my mind, this was my gift to him, a firstborn son, and I was honored to be able to be the vessel that carried this baby. Little did I know the journey that lie ahead.

In high school and college, I dated and lived the life of a typical teenage girl/young adult. Pizza, movies, football games, concerts, and proms littered the landscape of my limited (by my standards) social life in high school. In college there were parties, cabarets, step shows and balls – not to mention sorority life. My mind began to adapt to the idea of being in a long-term relationship; looking for THE ONE. There were times when I thought I had found "him", but reality always came crashing down, oftentimes with miserable, tearful results.

Then I made the decision that would change my life. My mentor, big sister, and cosmetologist, Deloris "Dee Dee" Freeman, invited me to the church that her husband Mike started pastoring while I was in college. I received Christ as a 16-year-old in their living room just a few years prior, and grew up in Mike's father's church, so it wasn't a far stretch for me. With all the partying and socializing I had done in college, she was always there to remind me of my foundation and kept me grounded. "Never forget your First Love," she would always caution me. During my senior undergraduate year, I decided to take her up on her offer and visited the church.

I visited and fell in love with the ministry and the Word of God that surrounded me like a blanket, protected and comforted me like a babe in the woods. I knew that this was where my spiritual home should be and that Pastors Mike and Dee Dee Freeman would be my spiritual parents. I was completely and totally head over heels in love with the ministry ...and then I met "him" – **the one**.

T. Gregory "Greg" Sothern, II was introduced to me by a mutual friend at church, and months later a second mutual friend suggested we spend some time together. We hit it off from the beginning. We were so very much alike, and yet so different. We both had been valedictorians at our respective high schools and received full scholarships to college. We both grew up in church. We both loved football, Scrabble, and intelligent conversation. Yet I was raised as an only child and he was one of 8 children. I lived in "the hood" and he lived in the suburbs. I had just graduated from college and he was still taking classes. Despite growing up in church, he knew **so much** about the Word and I knew so very little; but at that first telephone conversation, everything just clicked.

Fast forward again, 11 years – nearly seven years of dating (we called it "fellowshipping,") a home purchase, a career change and Master's degree for me, a new career as a firefighter/EMT for him, two miscarriages, along with hundreds of other life moments and milestones – we were now at the point of a new beginning. This pregnancy was fairly uneventful outside of a ton of indigestion (the older mothers would tell me that meant that my baby would have a lot of hair.) Granted, I conceived in March after having a miscarriage in January. I was concerned that it was too soon, but my obstetrician helped to ease my nerves. I was 33 years old having my first baby, but I had still not hit that milestone age of

35 where I would be considered AMA –
"Advanced Maternal Age."

My obstetrician (OB) was awesome – she was a
believer, (a Christian), and she belonged to
another church in my area. Her reputation was
legendary in the DC metropolitan area, and she
was considered one of the top obstetricians in the
region. She calmed my nerves by confessing the
Word when I needed it. She also helped me
understand what else my body was going
through that could have possibly led to my
previous miscarriages. She was always full of
information, encouragement, and lots of smiles.

When I was 22 weeks along, Greg and I went for
our routine anatomy ultrasound. We would finally
get a chance to see the first images of our baby
with all body parts (not the "shrimp" we saw at
week eight), and find out if we were having a girl
or boy. It was amazing to watch, and the
radiologists' first comment was "Wow, look at all
that hair!" (The mothers were right!) It was a boy!
The radiologist told us that she was having some
difficulty taking some pictures from the way he

was positioned. They tried to manipulate him to get him to move, but there he sat, with his arms behind his head as if to say, "I'm tired, let me relax!" Eventually she got the pictures she needed and we didn't think much of it - we chalked it all up to him being asleep.

Once we knew the baby was a boy we already knew what his name would be. We had always said that if and when we had a boy, we would name him after Greg and his father: Thomas Gregory Sothern, III, or "Tré" for "the third." Baby showers were next – our coworkers, friends and family were so happy for us. They knew our journey and about our previous losses, and this was a time of victory. We were abundantly blessed with gifts from our support system, our "villiagit seemed like everything was set for our new arrival.

Tré was due December 20, 2003. With six weeks to spare, the obstetrician noticed that he had not turned, causing him to be breech. Additionally, my blood pressure was elevated. She took note of the blood pressure and stated that we needed to watch it closely. When I went back in two more weeks my BP was still up and Tré was still not in position. The doctor suggested that we schedule a C-section, as she did not want me to work unnecessarily pushing him out during the birth and cause myself to develop preeclampsia. She asked us to choose between December 12th and December 19th as the delivery date. We figured the 19th would give us a bit more time, and was closer to his original due date. So the date was set -- our firstborn would come into this earth on Friday, December 19, 2003. What we didn't know was that our lives were about to take a drastic turn, and NOTHING about Tré's birth would be anything that we expected.

Chapter Two

Birth Day

Riding to the hospital with Greg driving, I was certainly nervous about having the C-section. I had not had surgery since I had my tonsillectomy when I was four years old. Who remembers an almost 30-year-old procedure? The butterflies that came on the big day were not just about the surgery, but even more so the life, the baby, the son we were about to bring into our lives. I went through the checklist in my mind before we left - car seat ... check ... going-home outfit ... check ... nursing supplies ... check ... mommy bag ... check ...

Thoughts about the baby's room that we decorated with the theme of my favorite children's author, Eric Carle, author of the classic story, "The Very Hungry Caterpillar," helped soothe my nerves. My good friend Sonya who had twin boys who were five years old and had outgrown their cribs, allowed me to use one of hers (we found that she was going to be needing the other one as she had a baby six months after Tré was born), and my mom purchased him a dresser and hutch that was full of "Onesies" sleepers, and tiny fresh smelling clothes in hues of blue, chocolate, and cream.

I spent December 18th putting up the Christmas tree. I figured I wouldn't be in much of a mood to deal with a tree when we came home. Since the C-section was on December 19th I calculated that I would be home by the 22nd, but I decided not to push it. I wanted everything to be nice and festive when we brought Tré home. By the day's end I was exhausted, but Greg and I capped off the evening by purchasing a video camera and taking in a late show to see the movie, "The Lord of the Rings: The Return of the King."

These images danced thought my mind as I leaned back in the seat next to Greg. It was a delightfully sunny day in December. Christmas décor whizzed by as we were on our journey. Many of our family members were hustling and bustling about preparing for the holidays. With six days to go before Christmas, there was much to be done (but at least the tree was up!) The "Grandmothers" – my mom, and Greg's mom and aunt – would all meet us at the hospital in anticipation of the baby.

We checked into the hospital in the Labor and Delivery department. After I had been dressed and laying on the bed the nurse asked me if I had been feeling any contractions. "No," I told her, to which she responded by showing me a series of mountains and valleys on the fetal monitor sheet. "Yes you are!" she declared. It was a surprise to me, but of course this was my first experience being at such a late stage of pregnancy so I had no clue what I was feeling. I gave hubby one last kiss as the transport technician came to get me to take me to the operating room, and assured that he would be ready with our newly-purchased video camera to document our big day.

I was wheeled into the operating room where I saw my OB and was introduced to the anesthesiologist. I was surprised at how cold the room was and they assured me that it was typical. I shivered a bit while the anesthesiologist opened the back of my loose hospital gown and found the exact spot for my spinal block. First I felt a pinch, then a little burn. I couldn't even get my legs up on the table because they numbed so quickly; the nurses had to help me. I laid back and got ready for the ride.

They continued to prep me for the procedure, and I became aware that my husband was not in the room. "Oh no," I thought, "He can't miss this!" I looked at the OB, "Where's Greg?" I asked her. She told the nurses to get him in there quickly. Good thing too – she moved fast! By the time Greg came rushing into the room with the video camera, she was pulling up the blue sheet that blocked my view of my lower body and starting the procedure by opening me up. As she worked, Tré began to appear: everyone commented on how much hair they could see on my new baby boy. A few pulls and he was out! After miscarriages and tears and pain, our Tré was finally here. At 6 lbs. and 9 oz., and 20 inches long, he was a good-sized baby. It was the moment we had awaited for years, but it wasn't quite what we expected.

I immediately noticed that Tré did not cry. He gave a few small squeaks and grunts, but no real cry. I couldn't see over the blue sheet. "What's going on, why isn't he crying?" Greg reassured me. "There still cleaning him up, and they're massaging him." Massaging him? I thought it sounded strange but I was a bit woozy from the medication and my mind was racing so I did not process that immediately. I waited for what seemed like a lifetime. Finally they wrapped him up, put the pink and blue cap on his shock of curly black hair, and presented him to me. "Here's your baby." I touched his face gingerly, then they whisked him away to the nursery.

"Wow, that was anticlimactic," I thought. But hey, this was my first baby, and I DID just have a C-section, so maybe this was standard.

So they wheeled me into recovery and my husband came with me. As we entered the room, I saw our three mother figures waiting in the hallway. I felt myself drifting in and out of consciousness. In what seemed like moments, my OB came in with that big smile on her face. I had gotten to know that smile very well over the past seven months, and it was a source of comfort and reassurance to me. I smiled back at her, and then she dropped the bomb:

"Well, the good news is, the baby's heart is strong ..."

I was a bit puzzled, wasn't it supposed to be strong? If that was the good news, then what else was there for her to tell us? I'm sure she saw the looks on our faces, so she went on,

"Your baby has a condition called Arthrogryposis. It basically means that all his joints are contracted and he is very tight. He was having some problems breathing but we think it's stabilized ..."

Everything else she said became a distant hum. I could hear her talking, but I wasn't focused on what she was saying. Waves of thoughts that were flying through my head. Through it I could hear phrases like "These kids have a great prognosis ..." and "... splints, casts, and surgeries." She gave us some written information she had printed for us from the Internet about the condition, "arthrogryposis multiplex congenita." What is that? I don't want to read about that; this is supposed to be a happy day. No, she must be mistaken. As she finished talking to Greg, I felt dizzy and disoriented. Was it the meds? I was trying to process it all, but I felt like my head was in a cloud.

When she left, our mothers flooded the room with loving arms and hugs. My mom reached me first and hugged me, "You okay Pookums?" "Yeah, I think so." I wasn't processing well. She rubbed my hand, but I could tell there was more that she wished she could do and say. I would learn that as a parent, you never stop wanting to protect your children no matter how old they get; but there are some things they are just going to have to experience for themselves. My "mother-in-love" was next, full of the Word, as usual. She reminded me about the story in the Bible when a man had an ailment, and the Jews asked Jesus if the cause was because of his parents' sin or a sin of his own. "Neither," Jesus answered, "But this is so that God would be glorified."

"Tré's condition is here so that God would be glorified!" She said it with so much encouragement and excitement that I loved her even more; but I just didn't want to hear that. I wanted a regular baby, not one with all these issues.

My Aunt Neta held my hands and looked in my eyes and told me, "God gave you this special baby for a reason – because you two are the best people to take care of him." Again, I loved her for her words of comfort but at the time it wasn't comforting.

Almost immediately, I needed to see him. I needed to hold him and touch him and verify with my own eyes what everyone was telling me, but I had to wait for what seemed like hours more to get a room. On a maternity floor with only four private rooms, my doctor made sure that I got one of them. Once I was in the room we had to wait even longer. The doctor came in to tell me that they were going to transfer Tré to Children's National Medical Center in Washington, DC. I delivered him at Southern Maryland Hospital in Clinton, MD - Not quite an hour's drive, but not down the street either. "I want to make sure you get to see him before he gets transferred," she promised.

My heart raced. "You mean my baby won't be here?" I thought. I would have to spend the next three days on a hospital floor full of mothers and babies without having my own. Getting through days and nights, listening to the siren-like wails of newborns and mothers trying to comfort them while dealing with the reality of my own empty arms was a thought more than I could bear at the time, so I re-focused my energies elsewhere. "How long will it be?" I pleaded with her. "Not much longer," she reassured me that flashed that familiar smile again. She would prove to be correct.

Tré was wheeled into my room in an incubator with all kinds of bells and whistles attached to it. His hat had been removed and I could see that full head of hair everyone had been talking about since the sonogram. It was full and thick like mine as a newborn. His face was also very hairy; my mom called it "peach fuzz" that seemed to naturally progress from his hair down to his face into his eyebrows. But he was beautiful. His eyes were closed and his tiny face had C PAP wrapped around it from ear to ear and meeting at his nose, giving him some oxygen support. I didn't realize it at the time, but thinking back on it I don't remember his body moving at all. He made none of the random, spontaneous movements that babies make with their arms, legs and hands.

There were about four people there from the Children's Hospital transport team. "Hi I'm Victor," one of the men spoke up, "I'm going to take care of your baby on the way. Just give me a call at this number in about two hours and I can update you." He offered me some paperwork with a phone number on it. "That's the number to the NICU (Neonatal Intensive Care Unit). We will probably call you first, but just in case." I thanked him and put the papers to the side. Greg, my doctor, the mothers, auntie, and the transport team were all crowded into my room. The nurses from the nursery invited me to touch him. I put my hand into the incubator port holes and into the built-in gloves. I gingerly ran my finger along his warm tiny leg. He looked so fragile and helpless. He looked so frail and I didn't want to break him so I quickly withdrew my hand. The transport team exchanged information with the nurses and gave us their goodbyes, and my brand new baby boy went out the door with them.

So there I sat, in my bed, on the maternity ward, with no baby. My doctor left and promised to see me again the next day. The mothers eventually filed out. Greg and I started the difficult task of making phone calls to announce the birth of our son while at the same time explaining to people why a visit to my room would not mean getting to see the baby. It was hard to explain the reasons why when we didn't have a full understanding ourselves, but we did the best we could.

That evening, Greg made sure I was settled and cared for, then left to go to Children's to be with Tré. He took the video camera and promised to call when he got there. By then we had already heard from the NICU letting us know that Tre was in and settled. He hugged me tightly and we prayed. We thanked God for our new son. We thanked Him that our son was healed from the crown of his head to the soles of his feet. We thanked Him that the fruit of my womb was blessed. And we thanked Him for the testimony of the miracles that would follow as a result of this birth. My husband looked me straight in my eyes and said, "I love you; you did such a great job. We've got this." I thanked him and kissed him as he walked out the door. I was finally able to lie down and take a nap.

Later that night as the fog from the anesthesia wore off, I woke up. Alone in my room, my heart broke and I wailed and sobbed in solitude.

Chapter Three

Reality

I spent the weekend recovering in the hospital, aching to see my newborn baby boy. That Friday night, the NICU called to tell me that Tré was having a hard time breathing so they had to intubate him and give him breathing assistance through a ventilator. Greg took a video of me reading "The Very Hungry Caterpillar" (my favorite children's book) to him. He returned to my hospital room with a baby blanket that was used to swaddle him. It brought with it the distinct fragrance of newborn, my newborn. By the time Sunday came my OB came to visit. She told me that she would be discharging me the next day (Monday), and that I should try to take it easy. "Be sure to take a wheelchair to the NICU," she admonished, "I don't know how far away from the elevators you might have to walk." She reminded me to take my pain meds and be careful. I agreed and promised to do just that.

The next day I was discharged, and Greg and I made a beeline for Children's Hospital. Greg, who had been there every night since Tre was born, had already talked to the doctors and told them I would be coming that Monday. It was funny arriving at Children's as a parent – I had been there more times than I wanted to think of as a child. We waited for what seemed like forever in line at the front desk to check in. Greg asked for a wheelchair and we were given one quite effortlessly. We rode the elevator to the third floor. When the doors opened, I was a bit surprised to see that the church chapel was on the same floor (I would later understand why it was so appropriate.) We traveled down the hall, around the corner, past long hallways, beeps, bells and clicks. Finally we arrived at the NICU. There was a big steel basin with pedals on the floor and instructions on how to properly wash your hands: at least three minutes, soap up to your elbows, be sure to get under the fingernails, etc. We went through the formalities, met the receptionist, and went through the doors.

It's really overwhelming and a bit intimidating to be in a NICU if you have never been there. It's even more difficult when you are the parent of one of those babies. When Tré arrived at Children's he was placed in an "isolette," which is basically a room that can be closed off so that the infant in the room does not come into contact with any other babies (this was to protect him as well as the other babies who are in the unit). There was one nurse named Pat who was assigned to two isolettes, Tré's and another baby's. This was considered level 5 care – the highest that is available for NICU babies. Nurse Pat showed me to the room where there was a gaggle of awaiting doctors, fellows and interns. They were polite enough to allow me to pass through so that I could be reunited with my little one, but they hung back awaiting a sign that it was okay to ask me the dozens of questions they had. I passed by them all and entered the room. The wheelchair wouldn't fit into the isolette so I stood up (I really didn't think it was necessary anyway). Nurse Pat stood next to the "crib" and motioned me to come forward. I was keenly aware of the lights, monitors, and constant beeps, but I forced myself to tune them all out to focus on him.

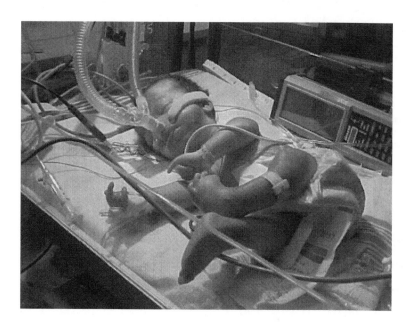

There he was, lying there in a napkin-sized diaper. He lay there so peacefully I didn't want to disturb him. I could see his tiny chest rise and fall, and I heard the ventilator hissing in sync with his breathing. That already infamous hair framed his angelic face. His eyes were closed and the nurse said he hadn't opened them. I was so busy looking at his face and trying to focus on it that I remembered I should look at his extremities. His fingers were long and thin (like mine) and they were tightly clasped together. His feet were bent and turned upward, pointing toward his face. When I had the ability to take in the entire scene, I crumbled.

Greg placed his hands around my shoulders, and the medical staff brought me a chair. I cried softly for a few minutes then I looked up and actually noticed that the doctors and staff were waiting to talk to me. I collected myself and gave them the signal to come forward. They asked what seemed like a thousand questions, and many of them I would hear time and time again as I took Tré to different appointments: How old are you? Do you have any other children? What's your pregnancy history? Was this a normal pregnancy? Did you have any complications? Did you make all of your prenatal appointments? What medicines did you take? How many weeks were you when you gave birth? Do you have any family history of anything of this type? Are you and your husband related? (that one really got to me.) Question after question, I answered as best I could: 33 … no … this is my third … yes … no … yes … none … 39 weeks and 6 days … no … absolutely not …

Over the next four weeks Greg and I spent our days visiting with Tré and trying to maintain some sense of normalcy at home. Tré opened his eyes on Christmas day, and Nurse Pat called me on my cell to tell me. It was bittersweet because I missed it, but the timing of the call was perfect because I was at home in tears depressed about not having my baby at home on his first Christmas. During that time, we began to get a clearer picture of what was going on with him.

Even though we had been told that Tré had Arthrogryposis, we learned that that was just a description of his body. There had to be an underlying reason that caused him not to move while he was in utero. The geneticists wanted to do blood tests on him to determine what the reasons were so they could give us a better idea of his prognosis. The neurologists wanted to make sure his brain was okay so they performed CT scans. The gastroenterologists wanted to make sure that his NG tube was cared for correctly. The pulmonary doctors wanted to be sure that his breathing was monitored and regular, especially after he got off the ventilator at two weeks; and the orthopedists – they needed to correct his clubbed feet through casts, and relieve the contractures in his hands with hand splints.

To be certain, the entire experience was overwhelming. When the doctors and specialists spoke about Tré they did not have voices that sounded sure of his recovery. It was more like "guarded optimism." They told us that we would probably need a lot of support when we took him home. They would be sure that the NICU Social Worker spoke with us before his discharge to make sure we had the resources we needed. It was probably the most helpless feeling I have ever had, I – who had been such a high achiever all my life and who, through God's help and my own sheer will, had been able to meet just about every goal I had set for myself – had to basically sit back and watch other people describe for me what they were doing to take care of **my** child. It seemed a bit unnatural and just not right.

Prayer was the most important thing we could provide for him. We had a network of "family," both immediate and extended, biological, church, work, and friends, who put their time and efforts into praying for our baby boy. Our pastors and church family at Sprit of Faith Christian Center were on it as soon as they got the word. The pastors at my "In-loves'" church had a prayer vigil for him. A parent of one of my first-graders, Pastor Liz Rodgers, put him on a 24-hour prayer watch for a week. Each day of that week someone at the church was praying for him every hour of the day. We, as his parents, of course had to pray. We prayed and thanked God for his healing, that he was healed from the crown of his head to the soles of his feet. That no weapon formed against him would prosper (Isaiah 54:17). That the fruit of my womb was blessed (Deuteronomy 28:4). That what the enemy meant for evil will turn out for good (Genesis 50:20).

That the testimony of his journey would be a blessing in the lives of many others. That he would live AND NOT DIE! And that he would be able to walk and run and function like other children. That we were not moved by what we saw but we would stand firm on the Word of God!

All the while I focused on what I could provide for him: milk. I became known on the NICU for producing a ton of milk. I heard whispers of "cow" and "wet nurse" floating around me. Since Tré had no gag, suck, or swallow, he had to be given a nasojejunal (NJ) tube, which eventually became a nasogastric (NG) tube. Both tubes were inserted through the nasal cavity, but the former goes directly into the intestine, and the latter goes into the stomach. This is where his milk, medicines and nutrients entered his tiny body. I then had to use a pump to produce milk, store it, then take it into the hospital where it was labeled and stored for his use. Thank God for my lactation consultant/pediatric nurse practitioner Kristal Tibbs (whom I affectionately referred to as "The Milk Nazi"), who let me call her in the middle of the night for advice.

"Kris, I'm sleepy and I'm SO TIRED, the nurse from the hospital told me I should just take a nap and pump (the milk) when I wake up."

"Absolutely not!" she answered, "If that baby were there at home, you would be getting up in the middle of the night to feed him every three to four hours. Set your alarm clock and get up and pump."

So that became my routine. No matter where I was - at church, at the family Christmas gathering, at the hospital, at the doctor's office, at home – I didn't let that stop me from being "super-milk-maid." By the time Tré was discharged I had a large Coleman cooler full of two-ounce milk bottles (Thanks Kris!). God bless my late grandmother Rhoda Smith who allowed me to store most of that milk in her deep freezer because we definitely didn't have room for it all.

Spending time in the lactation room in the NICU gave me the opportunity to meet other mommies whose babies were in the NICU for various reasons. One mommy had a baby with Spina

Bifida. Another had a baby with Cystic Fibrosis, and her milk had to be treated with a compound that allowed the baby to digest it properly. Another woman had given birth to twins, one who was left back at the hospital where she delivered causing her and her husband to have to split time between both hospitals. Still another mommy had twins prematurely after three trials of in vitro. One didn't survive, but the other one was fighting for her life.

Over the humming of breast pumps we exchanged stories about our pregnancies and newborns, and we formed a sort of involuntary sorority united by the most undesirable circumstances. By listening to the stories of so many women I was able to appreciate my own child's situation. I couldn't imagine having two babies in two different hospitals, or having to fight for one baby while mourning for another. I'm sure they felt the same about me, but that time gave me an appreciation of the power of perspective: being able to have a positive outlook at one's own situation and being grateful for the life you have, rather than being desirous of someone else's life.

Weeks passed and Tré had visitors – our parents and siblings, aunties and uncles. I remember Greg's mom, Patricia, coming to visit him for the first time and commenting, "He has intelligent eyes." I thought that was an odd comment, and wondered how in the world she could see that, but I also knew her well enough to know she was spiritually perceptive beyond measure and not to question it (I would remember that comment later on during a pivotal time). We also had great supporters – Kevin and Sonya Thomas who lived close by, and brought us food while we were at the hospital; Dr. Sophia Smith who worked at Children's in the Pediatric Intensive Care Unit (PICU) and gave us the ins and outs of the hospital as well as great spiritual advice coupled with medical advice (along with his first books and a bowl, cup and cutlery set!). We made friends while we were there with hospital staff of all vocations: nurses, people at the front desk, phlebotomists, cafeteria workers, etc.

Finally, around January 13th in the New Year 2004, the doctors told us that Tré would be coming home soon. We were equally excited and terrified! We were happy to finally bring him home like we wanted to for so long, but what would we do without all the help at the hospital? How would we be able to properly care for him with all of his needs? We had been able to assist with his care increasingly more as he grew and we were comfortable with the regular baby care – changing, dressing, and bathing were not a concern for us. It was the new stuff – feeding him with the NG tube, putting the splints on his hands, caring for those heavy casts that weighed his little legs down (the splinting and casting began while he was in the NICU to help straighten his hands and feet). How in the world would we be able to manage him?

The social worker assured us that we would be okay. She made sure that we had his first appointments scheduled. She gave us information on the Infants and Toddlers' Early Intervention Program for our county, and encouraged us to contact them as soon as possible. She also gave me a list of outpatient clinic appointments with the specialists that Tré had already seen at the hospital and that were scheduled for later on that month. They asked us to bring in his car seat the next day so they could place him in it and be sure his breathing could withstand sitting up – he passed the assessment with flying colors!

On January 15, 2004 (Dr. Martin Luther King Jr.'s birthday), on the 28th day of the life of Thomas Gregory Sothern III, he left Children's National Medical Center with his mommy and daddy. Before we left the hospital with him, we had been given a general impression about what they said his prognosis would be: we should consider the possibility of institutionalization, he would probably not be able to move much at all, his breathing would always be an issue for him, and they were not optimistic about his cognitive or physical development. No matter to us: Greg and I were so excited to be finally bringing him home we pushed all that to the back of our collective consciousness. Plus, we felt like we had an upper hand on his situation – surely with all the prayer that he had been bathed with over the past four weeks he was destined to beat the odds.

I sat with him in the back seat of our car and like every new mommy I watched his every movement on the way home. We brought him in the house and placed him under the Christmas tree. I refused to take it down before he came home; it seemed perfectly appropriate as we placed him there in the company of our family and friends who were awaiting his arrival, because he was truly the best gift we had ever received.

Chapter Four

Treading Water

Over the next few weeks our household adjusted to what I like to call "a new normal": Greg was assigned to his first fire station and was on a 24/72 hour rotating shift, so he worked for 24 hours and was off for 72 hours. I did not have to go back to work until March – I was granted eight weeks from my doctor but since I was a teacher, I was not charged the days that we were out for winter break or holidays. So between Greg and I, we filled our days with doctors' appointments, receiving visitors and guests, and getting used to being new parents. Tré was not like most newborns – he did not cry, and his face was almost expressionless. His eyes were always very alert, looking and watching everything. There is an old English proverb that says, "The eyes are the window to the soul." We would find that proverb to be true very soon.

Tré had his first visit with his new pediatrician; a kind older doctor who had a practice not far from us in Crofton, MD. The pediatrician we wanted and would eventually get was my lactation consultant/Certified Pediatric Nurse Practitioner Kristal, but she was on leave at the time of Tré's discharge, and the doctor we saw was her consulting physician. The first few trips were always a little complicated because of those casts. He couldn't get immunized until the casts came off because we couldn't get to his thighs. His weight was always incorrect because the casts were so heavy! At four weeks he was already behind on his immunizations coming out of the hospital but the doctor assured me that we could get him caught up without concern.

During that time, we also took Tré to the orthopedic ('ortho") clinic at Children's Hospital. It was during my first visit to the ortho clinic that I met the doctor assigned to Tré's case. She was one of the top surgeons in the division, well respected and admired. She always had three or four interns, fellows, and assistants with her and they followed her throughout the clinic like ducklings behind a mama duck as she visited and consulted with the many patients waiting to see her. She introduced herself to me and explained in detail everything that they observed to be problematic with Tré's skeletal structure: he had scoliosis (curved spine), bilaterally clubbed feet, and bilaterally dislocated hips, among other things. She then began to tell me all of the things she and her team would do to correct those issues, but I noticed she didn't say anything about his hips. "What about his hips?" I asked, "Won't it be difficult for him to walk if his hips are out of joint?"

"We weren't expecting that he would be doing much walking."

"Whoa, wait a minute," I thought. "What does that mean?" I guess she saw the question in my eyes and went on. She told me how a surgery leaves scar tissue and that since Tré was not going to be walking (in her opinion), the presence of the scar tissue would make his hips very stiff and inflexible. It was a surgery that was not worth the risk if he was not expected to be walking anyway.

Her words had a delayed effect. I don't think I understood the full gravity of what she was saying until I got home later that day. I remember nodding and listening to her explain how the process of serial casting works. I didn't have time to stop and process it because there was so much more information to gather. Since Tré's feet were "clubbed" (imagine a foot looking like a golf club), they would take off his casts, stretch his feet outwards, then cast him again with his feet stretched. Every four to five days I would have to bring him back to get new casts and more stretching. The goal was to increase the flexibility in his ankles and to place his feet into a weight-bearing position. After six weeks she would do a tendon release in which she would snip his Achilles tendon and do a final stretching of his feet into the ideal position. Then she would cast him and he would have to keep those casts for another six weeks. I was nervous about the surgery on my little baby as one could imagine, but I didn't have time to think about it. I placed it "on the shelf" in my memory; I just needed to get through and manage my current situation.

On February 5, 2004 (my birthday), Tré had his very first outpatient surgery. I would be lying if I said I wasn't nervous, he was only six weeks old and still so tiny and seemingly fragile. By this point, we had seen doctors in Genetics and Neurology. The neurologist suggested a muscle biopsy to determine if his lack of movement was attributed to some type of congenital muscle defect. If that were the case, the doctors had very little hope that his situation would improve. It was determined that the biopsy would be done at the same time as the tendon release, so as to get both procedures done at the same time. The procedure was over quickly, and we brought our baby back home, not to return to the ortho clinic until mid-March.

Valentine's Day came soon after, and Greg and his siblings decided to visit his maternal grandfather. Horace B. Johnson was a legend and one of Greg's personal heroes. At the time he was blind, and his health was declining, but he was still living at home so we thought it was important for him to have a visit with his youngest great-grandchild. When we went to see him and placed the baby in his arms, he surprisingly said, "He's so heavy!" We explained to him that the baby had casts but it didn't matter to him. The love that was in his eyes was present even though his vision was not. It would be the first and only time he would get to see Tré.

One of the tasks I was able to complete during that first month home with Tré was getting early intervention services. As an educator, I knew the importance of getting children the help they need as soon as possible; I would learn that on an even deeper level as a mommy. I got in touch with the parent of another one of my first-grade students and asked her for information on how to get services for Tré. She connected me to someone, who connected me to The ARC of Prince George's County (which I found out later was the same information the NICU social worker had given me). The ARC provides case management for the Infants and Toddlers program for our county. I called and asked for an assessment. After giving them our discharge papers from the hospital, in addition to answering a laundry list of questions about prenatal health and his development thus far, they were able to arrange a home visit with a case manager, a special education teacher and a physical therapist.

The case manager, Jill, came with Sue, the physical therapist and Susan, the special education teacher. They did their respective assessments: Sue did the physical assessments, looking at muscle tone and development; and Susan did the cognitive assessments, which looked at his ability to track and recognize my voice, among other things. We fell in love with both Sue and Susan immediately. They were encouraging and warm, but also very professional. Children qualify for services if they are more than 25% delayed in their developmental milestones. Since he was 8 weeks old, he would qualify if he scored anything less than 6 weeks. Since he had no independent movement he definitely qualified based on his physical development. However, Susan observed something that a lesser teacher would not have noticed. "He turned his eyes towards your voice," she mentioned as I walked throughout my living room and talked to them. "He knows his mommy's voice." I was shocked and didn't quite understand the significance of that statement until later, (remember the "intelligent eyes comment?) What I would come to find out later is there is always more going on inside Tré than what the normal person could observe. It takes special and talented people to not only be able to see his potential, but also draw it out of him. His eyes truly were, and still are, a "window" to his soul!

A few weeks later we had another meeting where we set up a plan for Tré's services. We developed an "Individualized Family Services Plan," or and IFSP. As a teacher, I knew what an IEP was and I was told the two documents were very similar. An *IFSP* is for children from birth – 3 years old, and revolves around the family, since it is the only constant a child has in their life. An *IEP* is for children three years old and up, and strictly revolves around the student, because it's the child's education that is being discussed. Tré would have physical therapy three times a month and a visit from the teacher for academic services once a month. We also found out that both Sue and Susan would be providing Tré with those services and we were so excited because we had really grown fond of them both. As the months progressed, we became dependent on their input and feedback as they gave us advice. That information helped us not only meet Tré's physical needs, but also helped our family get adjusted to this unique situation in which we found ourselves.

Around the first of March it was time for me to go back to work. Having Tré just before the winter break, in addition to the Martin Luther King Holiday and Presidents' Day gave me an extra 12 days on top of my eight-week break mandated by my C-section. Like any mother, I was nervous about leaving my newborn, my first-born, to return to the workplace. Tré's situation made me feel even more protective than normal, (at least I thought so), but much of the uncertainty I would have felt was alleviated by the fact that we had recruited someone to care for him that would have nothing but his best interests at heart – my "mother-in-love", Patricia Sothern.

I went back to work, and faced the relentless questions and comments from colleagues, students, and parents: "How's the baby?" "Is he home yet?" and, "Ooh, I saw his pictures!" (Someone sent pictures of him by way of email to my friends and coworkers. I wasn't happy about that, but I had to let it go.) Eventually, I was able to settle in and get back into the groove of classroom instruction.

Chapter Five

The Cocoon

I had always been somewhat offended by Tré's orthopedist saying she was not expecting him to "do much walking" (let me be clear, I absolutely love and respect her as a doctor). I understood that doctors have to give a prognosis based on their experiences, but to make that type of statement, to me, was unconscionable. I probably acted as if I were in a bit of denial, and looking back on it, I am glad I did.

Through a flurry of specialists' appointments, Greg and I learned that Tré would need several more surgeries, including one to repair a hernia, and one to place a gastrointestinal tube (G-tube) into his belly. We were still awaiting the news about whether or not he could get the hip surgery, which in our eyes, was the most crucial one. Once we got the last set of casts off he was given splints. They looked like casts but were open in the middle. We followed the directives of the doctor – we kept him in his splints 23 hours a day. And during bath time we put him in the tub and tickled his tiny little feet. What happened after that would become the substance of Sothern family folklore.

One night I put Tré down for bed in his crib, and I turned around to get some clothes from his dresser. Out of the corner of my eye I saw something move; I turned around, and he was looking at me with those eyes. Then I saw it – he was lifting his legs in the splints! "Oh my goodness," I thought. Then I tried to convince myself that I didn't see it when sure enough -- he did it again!

"The doctor is not going to believe this," I thought; but seeing his little legs lift those heavy splints up made me even more determined. We all massaged and moved and tickled his legs and feet until he was actually kicking his legs. We were all excited and couldn't wait until the next appointment with the orthopedist.

Greg's grandfather passed away around the same time Tré's splints were to come off. I had already returned to work, and Greg was off the day of the appointment so he took the baby to see the doctor. We agreed to meet that afternoon at the funeral home for the family viewing, as it was the day before the funeral. I told Greg to make sure the orthopedist knew and saw that he was kicking. When he came back, Tré's splints were gone and were replaced by a pair of shoes attached to a bar (a "foot abduction brace"). We had to follow the same routine as with the splints – 23 hours on, one hour off; and she wanted us to continue to work on his legs and feet. Not a problem at all; we were to go see her again in three months.

In April during Easter week, Tré got an infection and had to be hospitalized for a few days. His first Easter Sunday was spent at the hospital (later on we noticed that we seemed to have hospitalizations around major holidays!) We never figured out exactly what caused the infection, but were happy when it was time to go home. The next month, he had his second surgery to place a G-tube in his tummy. That was a relief as we were finally able to take the feeding tube off his face, where the adhesive bandage that was used to keep it in place was constantly irritating his skin. The world was finally able to look at his face, and see him as a "regular" baby. Good or bad, that was important to me. We scheduled his first professional pictures and his baby dedication for June.

In June we revisited the orthopedist. She was again shocked to see that not only was Tré kicking, but he was rolling over! "I think it's time to schedule that hip surgery," she relented. "Yes!" He would finally get the surgery that will send him on the road to being able to walk. But what did that mean? We now had more questions than ever before.

Over the next few months we spent time developing a relationship with Tré. I was home for the summer for the first time since I started teaching seven years prior. Therapy, first smiles, and a noticeable love for music were all a part of that season. A hernia surgery was the big news of the month of June, along with our fifth wedding anniversary, and Tré's baby dedication at church with a corresponding family cookout at my mom's house. We also spent the first six months trying to catch up on all of his immunizations. That time was really precious for me, and gave me even more opportunity to bond with my baby boy. It was a good thing too, because August was coming. I didn't realize that the events surrounding his hip surgery would send me careening once again on another roller-coaster ride of parenting this exceptional baby.

When August arrived, we took Tré in for his biggest surgery to date. Considering he had already had a few at that point, we were expecting it to be unremarkable. Honestly, I really don't remember many of the details about it (maybe I have repressed some memories). It was a blur of unexpected twists and turns. What was supposed to be a routine bilateral hip reduction ended up being a two week adventure of highs and lows, including a visit to the Pediatric Intensive Care Unit (PICU), an education on the effects of sepsis (infection of the blood), long days and nights of not understanding why my perky, happy baby, who had just recently showed us his first social smile, was asleep for three days, and unable to stir or be awakened. Prayers, tears, and conversations with doctors, all melded into one big ball of memories. What I do remember is taking him home with a full body cast, (from waist to ankle), and a short supply of preemie diapers which were to be tucked on the inside of the cast, and size 5 diapers to cover the outside of the cast. We were to see the orthopedist in three months to get the cast removed. It would be a long autumn.

August became September, which drifted into October and on to November. Those three months were challenging to say the least. Finding clothes appropriate for him to wear with the cast was an issue (big Onesie tee-shirts were best). Also, keeping the inside of the cast clean and dry was more difficult than the outside! Between the pee and the poop, a portable hair dryer and baby wipes became my best friends.

Carrying him around became another challenge. He was already nice and healthy – chubby for a baby, but add to that the weight of his cast. I can say we all got some good strength training in during those months! Trying to lift the car seat for car trips, explaining to strangers and friends what the cast was for, and dealing with the awkwardness of it all became another issue in and of itself. We were able to get his casts cut after two months, and that gave us the opportunity to take care of his skin on his lower legs which had begun to break down under the cast.

Just before Thanksgiving, we took Tré back to the orthopedist to get the cast removed. Back to the cast room again, listening to the whirring of that saw and the "cast lady" do her best to distract kids who were upset by the loud noises with her cries of "Whee!" and "Whoopie!" I watched very closely as she cut Tré's cast open and he emerged like a butterfly from a cocoon. I hadn't seen his little legs in their entirety in three months, and his skin had begun to break down. I immediately attacked it with Eucerin, and made a mental note to have a good bath ready for him when we got home. She wanted us to get him fitted for some orthotic braces that went up to his knees that would give more support in his ankles and legs. We scheduled that appointment on the way out the door. In the interim, it was time for our first official family pictures.

In late November my little family of three went into the studio with three outfit changes and I was so excited and proud to be finally taking professional family pictures! Tré was adorably round and plump, with a juicy mouth full of erupting teeth and an afro that would rival any from the '70s era. Greg was as handsome and stylish as ever, and I was completely overwhelmed at how good God had been to us over the past year. They let us view and select the poses an hour after the shoot was over, and we came home with way more pictures and poses than should ever be allowable. Family pictures were a success. It was now time to plan for the upcoming Christmas holiday and Tré's first birthday.

We decided to make Tré's birthday an extended family dinner/celebration. We felt that our family and friends were critical getting through that crucial first year, and we had to include them in the celebration. On Saturday December 19, 2004, our townhouse was overflowing with family, friends, and well-wishers. Food, music, and fun all provided the backdrop to a gathering that was the perfect ending to a year that could be described as eventful to say the least. We shared smiles, laughs, tears, and played an informal game of "pass the baby" (which consisted of Tré being passed from person to person). Many of them had not seen him since he had gotten out of his full body cast, and they made the standard-but-genuine comments about how much he had grown, how great he looked, and how much of a miracle his life was. He was truly transforming right before our very eyes.

We had overcome so many obstacles to get to that point. God blessed us with the son we wanted for so long, but the circumstances surrounding his birth and first year were not at all what we expected they would be. Getting through the first year of his life provided us with the strength we would need to face even greater challenges and battles in the next few years.

ADVICE & ADVOCACY

The purpose of the second part of this book is to help parents and caregivers navigate the waters of having an infant with special needs. I pray that it will also be useful to **all** who are caring for a loved one of any age and need suggestions on how to manage different elements of their collective journeys. I will give advice based on my experiences and information I have gained over the years and from other parents and professionals. The information is both specific and generic, so one should remember to use it as an outline and customize it for your own family circumstances, where appropriate.

Chapter Six

Managing Spiritually

There is no way we would have been able to get through Tré's first year had we not been spiritually grounded; it was crucial. When you go through a life challenge there must be something you can hold onto that is bigger than yourself, something that will give you peace in the very center of the storm that is swirling around you. For Greg and me that part was a no-brainer – we were both infused with faith-based teaching as young children, but as adults we gained deeper knowledge from our pastors.

We had been taught long before we had Tré that Faith came by hearing and hearing the Word of God (Romans 10:17). We had to look at that baby and find out what the Word said about healing and what God promised us as believers and as His children. He said the fruit of my womb was blessed! (Deuteronomy 28:4) He said that He (Jesus) came that we might have life and have it more abundantly! (John 10:10) He said that He wished above all things that we prosper and were in health! (3 John 1:2) He said that when Jesus was beaten and crucified on the cross, He took on those 39 stripes so that healing could be ours! (Isaiah 53:5) How could we not expect anything else but healing to take place? Sure, what we saw initially may not have looked like healing, but we knew that through prayer – asking Him for what we wanted according to His Word, and then continually thanking Him for doing just that (even if it didn't look like it at that time) – we could have that for which we prayed.

Confess the Word over your baby or loved one. Don't operate in denial and act like there is no issue/challenge there. Don't be "spooky" and say things like, "There's nothing wrong with him/her." The Bible says we "call those things that be not as though they were," not the other way around (calling things which are as though they are not). Say what God says about him/her, "The Bible says you are healed by the stripes of Jesus, and that we overcome by the word of our testimony!"

So for all of you who are reading this, if you do not know what God says about healing, about your children, your family, or about what His promises are, I have given you some specific verses but spend time reading the Word and finding out for yourself. Find some books that talk about healing. I suggest you go to your local Christian bookstore and ask them for recommendations. Get yourself into a good Bible-based, Bible-teaching church that will not only inspire you on Sundays but empower you to live your life Monday through Saturday. You're going to need the "meat" of the Word of God that will sustain you, and hold you when you're not within the four walls of the church.

Also, guard your heart and your ears against well-meaning, well-intentioned family, friends, professionals and strangers who make innocent comments that actually could cause you to uproot the words you are speaking over your child or loved one. Things like, "Oh, God made him/her like that to make you stronger/teach you a lesson ..." No, God says He has healing in His wings (Malachi 4:2). Sickness is not a part of His nature. Or you may hear, "He/she will never walk/talk/etc." (I heard that one a lot.) You can very politely let it go in one ear and out the other. Continue to treat your baby as if you expect that he/she will be a typically developing child and watch the Word change the situation. WE chose to take the medical interventions (surgeries, therapies, casts, splints, and medications), that were suggested to us by the medical professionals, we continued to believe that he would get stronger, hit his developmental milestones, and that one day he would no longer need those interventions. Words are powerful – don't allow someone else's experiences and beliefs become yours.

Believe the Word.

Chapter Seven

Managing the Marriage

Statistics show that the divorce rate among parents of special needs children is 80%. That's 30% more than the general divorce rate of 50%. Why so high? Married couples who care for and nurture these special babies face a unique set of circumstances that many are ill-prepared to handle. My goal is to provide you with a few things to remember for both husbands and wives.

When Greg and I had Tré we had been married for four years. We had lots of opportunity to grow together as husband and wife, to work out the kinks, and to ensure that our marriage was really strong before we had children. Again, our pastors have established a strong marriage ministry so we had a foundation that was so strong, when this storm hit it did not tear our house down. That's not to say that the house didn't shake, reel, lose tiles and windows, etc. There was some damage done, but it was superficial; nothing that couldn't be repaired when calmer weather came.

If that is not the case for you and your spouse and your marriage is not as solid as you think it should be, I would advise you to IMMEDIATELY seek counseling. Think of your marriage as a chair, and that chair has to be strong enough to support the weight of your child. If the chair is rickety, ill-constructed, or otherwise unstable, your baby will fall and get hurt. Do not waste any time contemplating whether or not you should take that step. Your child's growth and development will be directly related to the strength of your marriage.

For Husbands/Daddies: Men are providers and protectors by nature. Their first instinct is to protect their seed and provide for it. When challenges come to their children many men feel helpless, and/or unable to do what God has ordained them to do from the beginning. Men, do not allow this situation be a pronouncement of your ability to do your job. Shift your thinking to the spiritual realm. What you may not be able to do physically you can do spiritually. Take the opportunity to be that praying Daddy who can protect his child with the words of his mouth. Doing so is even more effective than anything you can do for the child physically. As well, continue to protect the heart of your wife. Give her an ear and listen if she wants to vent, knowing you might not be able to "fix it." Put your arms around her and console her, let her feel the strength of your touch. She seeks safety and reassurance in your arms. (I recently read that extended hugs release the hormone oxytocin, which is associated with bonding, decreased blood pressure, and wound healing among other benefits). Pray for her in front of her, let her hear you building her up and protecting her with God's Word. Be willing to jump in and accompany and/or take the baby to the various and sundry specialists' appointments. Jump in and help with any exercises or protocols the therapists may prescribe for your child. Take the initiative and show her that you are just as invested in seeing your child grow and develop as she is. Let your words and deeds show her know that she is not alone, because she will be tempted with the thoughts that she is.

For Wives/Mommies: Pregnancy is designed to make women more sensitive to the needs of our children. From the moment we find out we are expecting our entire existence revolves around that child. What we eat, what we wear, where we go, the way that we sleep – it is all affected by that life growing inside us. When the baby is born, that symbiotic relationship continues even though the baby no longer resides inside us. We are keenly aware of the baby's needs and every cell within us is programmed to respond to those needs until they become intuitive - without thought or effort. THIS IS NOT THE CASE FOR MEN!! Do not expect them to "just know." They need a lot of support in knowing how to support you. It could be easy for us to turn inward when our husbands are trying to help and can't do things the "right" way. The first thought you have is, "Never mind, I'll do it myself!" You're robbing your child of the opportunity to bond with his/her father – this will be crucial in later years, so it is good to start early. Take the time to teach him how to change diapers, care for splints, dispense medications, practice physical therapy, etc. Eventually he will get the hang of things and will be able to relieve you of a few of the thousands of things that are all running through your head at the same time.

The biggest challenge I have seen of mothers with special needs children are they often feel isolated and alone. Men are not big talkers, especially when compared to women. When things settle down, take the time to find some support groups that will give you a listening ear. For some, talking to family members and friends might be difficult if you do not think they understand where you are coming from, but do not dismiss their advice without seeing if there is some value in it. Many times, the people who know us well and love us can be objective enough and knowledgeable enough to give us valuable feedback.

As a couple, remaining united about how you approach the situation is key. You must be in unity, having one voice and on one accord. The importance of communication cannot be understated. You may have to come up with some kind of game plan while you are still in the midst of chaos. "This is what we are going to say," or "This is how we deal with people" are a part of the discussion. Most importantly, find time to spend together alone, even if it's sitting alone on the couch watching a movie. You have to make an effort to maintain your relationship; it will not succeed if you leave it to itself. Everything in nature moves towards chaos; it is up to us to keep things in order and maintain peace. That's why God gave Adam the job to "dress and keep" the Garden of Eden. Even though God created it to perfection, a husband/tender was needed to keep it in order because He knew that as things grew they would get out of order. Your marriage is the same way. You must actively maintain it.

This is not about you; this is about the testimony that you will have together as a couple, and as a family and about the lives that will be changed as a result of hearing your story.

Chapter Eight

Managing Professionally

I am a full-time mom. I also work a full-time job outside my home. I make no apologies about working, and I love what I do. Someone recently asked me, "You didn't have to stop working when you had him?" No I did not. I understand that many people, specifically women, do not have that option. As I sated before, I gave birth to Tré in December and went back to work in March. By the time it was time for me to return to work I felt a tremendous amount of guilt about leaving him. There he was, vulnerable and defenseless (in my eyes) and I felt like I was abandoning him (somewhat). It didn't matter that he was staying with his grandmother, who I knew would do an outstanding job of caring for him in my absence; but still he was MY baby, MY responsibility.

I very quickly reconciled my feelings with my reality: my family stability required a two-person income (our household income disqualified him for Social Security benefits); and with mounting doctors' bills, co-payments for a variety of specialists, coupled with back-to-back appointments, our health insurance, which was tied to my job, was non-negotiable. In fact, we had to also opt-in to Greg's health insurance as secondary coverage because we couldn't keep up with the co-pays. (Now with the secondary coverage we very rarely EVER pay anything for medical costs.)

One of the things people always point to when discussing the teaching profession is the summer breaks. "Oh you're so lucky because you get three months off for the summer." First of all this is untrue. With the dozens of extra hours worked per pay period, between staying at work late, and bringing work home in the evenings and on weekends, the summer days are more like comp time. Even so, summers did provide me with opportunities to focus on specific skills for Tré that I would not otherwise have in a traditional 9 to 5, twelve month, 40 hour per week job. I spent that first summer of his life just getting to know him and developing a relationship with him, and boosting his social development. I was rewarded that August when he gave us his first social smile!

My advice on handling professional responsibilities would be for you to do what works best for your family; but as with anything else, you must first count the costs. If you have to temporarily (or permanently) stop working, then do that; but realize there will be certain sacrifices that your entire family will have to make. Some you will know on the front end, and some you won't find out until after you are already in the midst of your decision. What does that mean for your medical benefits? How will the financial ramifications affect your household?

If you are like me, and you cannot make the choice to leave, then there are other sacrifices you will have to make. One of the things that I missed the most was the special moments. I was usually at work when the therapists and teachers came to the house to work with Tre'. I would have to get the follow up information from my mom-in-love or through the write-ups that they left at home. Moms, don't be afraid to send your child to the doctor with Daddy! Because of his rotating schedule my husband took him to doctors' visits as Tré got older. I just didn't have the leave to use, and when I did I didn't have the flexibility because I am a teacher (it takes more effort to take a day off than it does to just stay at work). I would generally send Greg with a small notebook that listed all of Tré's medications and doctors' names for reference (our "Baby Bible"). I also wrote my questions for the doctors, and asked him to write down the answers. Now, that's not to say that I didn't get frustrated with the results in the beginning. I would get upset when he wouldn't ask follow-up questions or do things I thought should be easy to see, but I grew to realize that he had to get used to thinking like a caregiver. Once I got comfortable, I used his schedule to our advantage, and made appointments on days that I knew Greg would be off work. There was also a lot of organization that was required, as I had to synchronize Greg's and my work calendar with Tré's appointment calendar.

Having support from my colleagues was key as well. Many people were very curious to know exactly what happened when Tré was born. They had gotten bits and pieces, but never the full story. I have always been an open book, and if people asked me about him, I was always honest and willing to answer. Many people feel hesitant to ask about the baby's condition because they don't want to be offensive. Your baby is your heart, and the situation may be difficult for you to discuss, so share as much as you feel comfortable with, but do your best to make them feel at ease about asking you. You definitely don't want to burn any bridges and you just might need those colleagues to support you when you have an emergency and need to take some time off.

Above all, be professional. If you choose to work outside your home, allow your work ethic to shine in the workplace. As much as possible, confine your "second job" of Dr. Mommy to your break times and after your official work hours end. If you find your child's health management to be so overwhelming that your production declines or you can't keep up the pace, it may be time for you to evaluate if working outside your home is feasible for you. Remember, your child's care is your top priority

Chapter Nine

Managing Services

When I mention services, I am talking about all the people you need to interact with and things that you need to do in order to provide support to your baby/loved one: doctors, therapists, teachers, etc. Again, everyone's situation is different.

When Tré was first born he had a primary care physician, an orthopedist, a physiatrist, a neurologist, a gastroenterologist, a nephrologist, a urologist, an ophthalmologist, and a geneticist – and that's just the doctors. He also had two physical therapists (one through the school system, and one through the hospital), an occupational therapist, and a teacher who provided academic services. Coordinating appointments and services almost felt like a full time job in and of itself. As I started to feel myself go under from the weight of it all, my mom came up with a great solution.

She bought me a little notebook (remember the "Baby Bible"?) The front of the notebook had a little pocket where I kept his insurance cards. On the back cover I listed the names, specialties and phone numbers of all the doctors whom we frequented the most. Inside the book I took notes at appointments for personal reference – weight and length, suggestions from the physician, personal notes or whatever. I used this notebook to write down questions I had for the doctor when I sent the baby with Greg (or just so I would remember to ask them when I got to the appointment). Keeping this "journal" was useful to so I could reference what was said at other appointments and/or pass along doctors' information to other doctors. It saved my life!!

Our various specialists would mail us write-ups (dictations) from appointments for our records. We kept all those papers inside one central binder. Those notes were crucial whenever we were visiting a new doctor who wanted Tré's history. It was too much to commit to memory! We still have those notebooks to this day; I refuse to throw them away (and it's a good thing too; I recently had to access that old information when filling out paperwork for an intake program.)

Now let's talk about early intervention services. Being an early childhood education teacher, I was already a big supporter of early intervention. I know that the earlier a parent gets support for a child the better off he/she will be in the long run. So when we were discharged from the hospital the first thing I did was reach out to some parents who I knew had special needs children. One of my first grade parents gave me the phone number to a young lady at The Arc of Prince Georges County. I later found out that they coordinate the case management of the Infants and Toddlers Early Intervention Program in our county. The ARC works in conjunction with the Prince George's County Public Schools system. The Service Coordinator who works for The ARC, is the liaison between the families and the school systems. She made the arrangements for a teacher and physical therapist to come out and do the initial evaluation as well as all reassessments.

Once we had the assessment, and the results were reviewed, we were given the opportunity to accept or deny services. When we accepted services, the team (parents, teacher, specialist and service coordinator) developed an Individualized Family Service Plan (IFSP). This plan looked at individual goals for Tré's development from the family perspective. It focused on creating learning opportunities in everyday routines and activities, and was updated every 6 months. It is different from the more familiar Individualized Education Plan (IEP), which strictly revolves around the student and the child's education.

The Infants and Toddler's Program is Federally mandated through the Individuals with Disabilities Education Act (IDEA) and exists in every state and local jurisdiction. Children ages 0 through 2 with a suspected developmental delay are eligible for screening and assessments to identify early intervention needs in the areas of speech/language; physical, cognitive, and psycho-social development, and self-help skills. Services are provided at no cost to the family.

Services include:

- Special instruction
- Speech pathology and audiology
- Occupational Therapy
- Physical Therapy
- Psychological services
- Case Management
- Medical services for diagnosis
- Health services related to other early intervention services
- Family education, counseling, and support

To find out the organization that provides case management where you live, contact the hospital where you delivered your baby (or where your baby was discharged) and ask to speak to the social worker of that unit. If that doesn't work, search your state's department of education's website using the search term "infants and toddlers" or "early intervention." Your local Social Security Administration should also be able to give you contact information.

Chapter Ten

Managing Support

When Greg and I first found out we were pregnant with Tré, we reviewed all the child care options in our head like any couple with both spouses working. Greg suggested his mom, but I did not want to assume or impose. I was aware that even thought she was a stay-at-home mom, she had already raised eight children of her own and might not want to be tied down to a baby. Greg eventually posed the question to her, telling her that we would pay her, and she said she would get back to him. She responded that she would love to take care of her first grandchild and we were ecstatic!

During the first 11 weeks of Tré's life Grandma Pat was there – watching, learning and loving. She was a willing student when learning how to care for him.

She learned how to feed him, how to administer medications, how to exercise his limbs. When Sue and Susan (his first teacher and physical therapist), came for the first assessment visit she was there, as she would be the person home with him for most of their visits. Most of all, she loved him (and still does) beyond measure and bathed him constantly with her prayers and confessions. She was the one who instantly could see what was going on behind those eyes. By the time I was ready to go back to work, I was confident and comfortable with leaving him in her care.

For the next two years she not only cared for him, but also went above and beyond what any other caregiver would have done. She communicated information from the service providers when we returned home. She took him to appointments for various doctors and therapists. She prayerfully watched over him during hospital stays. She even took our baby home with her on Thursdays and kept him until Sunday afternoons! She was definitely instrumental in supporting us with the day-to-day care with the precious little baby we had been given.

As I mentioned in the previous chapter, my mother, with her gift of management and administration, assisted me with keeping my life from flying into a great big ball of chaos, and generally helped me keep my head screwed on correctly. Managing appointments, supplies, and scheduling all activities became an instantaneous juggling act. Tré was visiting so many specialists that I began to lose count. My mind was spinning along with my post-baby hormones. My mom gave me practical solutions to help me keep it all together while assuring me that I was doing a great job. She told me later that she was MY mother, and just like she knew I would make sure my baby was cared for, it was still her job to make sure her baby was cared for. Helping me organize was a big part of helping me stay mentally healthy so that I could take proper care of Tré.

My best friend Kisha was a great source of reassurance as well. We have been close since freshman year at American University, and she and her husband Lorenzo graciously volunteered to be Tré's godparents. Prayers, laughter, late-night phone calls, and the best birthday and Christmas gifts ever – she proved herself over and again to be a true friend from day one.

Other family members and friends were an integral part of our support network as well. From my grandmother allowing me to store my breast milk in her deep freezer, to my sister-friend Jeannelle watching Tré for a few hours to allow Greg and I a bit of down time, to my sister-friend Vonda being there for all his surgeries and hospitalizations, to our Aunt Neta coming over to help us do some "deep house cleaning," we have never lacked support from our circle of extended family and friends. We have always confessed the Word that says, my God will supply all my need (Philippians 4:19). We were able to see that firsthand through the loving and kind acts of those who were nearest and dearest to us.

Our church network was a great support to us as well. Our pastors, Dr. Mike and Dee Dee were always keeping us in prayer and making sure that we were spiritually strong. Other leaders in the church were there to assist us in getting and staying comfortable while we were there with equipment, special seating, etc. The leadership and members of our music ministry helped us adjust to our "new normal," embraced Tré into the family and gave us the ability to continue to serve for many more years after having him (his participation in our music department activities and rehearsals would prove to be very important in his language development down the road).

When it comes to getting support for yourself, remember this – you are NOT a bad parent because you need help! Having a new baby is one of the most wonderfully disorienting events in a family's life and it affects everyone in the household ESPECIALLY the mother, who is the primary caregiver. Additionally, hormonal and physiological changes affect our "mommy-brains." Our thinking and organizational skills are impacted, and the sleep deprivation only makes things worse. Add to that the additional layer of dealing with developmental issues that may or may not have been expected prior to giving birth and having to problem-solve and think "on the fly" amidst this situation that for most of us, is not ideal. Take help in whatever form it comes, and ASK for help when (not if) you need it.

Many of the people in your circle want to help, but may not know how to help. Look for family and close friends who can give you a hand. If you need to, create a list of household things that need to be done – laundry, dishes, cleaning, homework help or baby-sitting if you have other children, grocery shopping, etc. The duties do not necessarily have to involve your special needs infant. When people come to you and say, "Call me if you need anything," or "Whatever I can do to help you just let me know," you can respond with, "Yes I REALLY need some help with (insert chore here), can you look at your calendar and let me know when you can come over?"

Call those people to action! You will see that they will either jump in and surprise you, or you will find that they were asking rhetorically and can't or won't genuinely be able to help you (it doesn't mean you break ties with them, they just may be unable to help).

Additionally, seek support within your community from church groups, civic associations, etc. One way to do this is to let your fingers do the Internet walking. Use your child's diagnosis as a search term to seek support groups but beware of some of the images and visuals you will invariably see during your search on the Internet and social media. Also, be sure to screen your "support" groups – some of them become a haven of people who want to complain about their situations. Sometimes people need to vent, but always be careful to protect your eyes and ears against things that will plant negativity into your heart and put you in a different frame of mind as it refers to your child. If you consistently feel worse after dealing with a group, it's not the one for you.

Support groups are, however, a great place to seek encouragement from people who are in situations similar to yours. Oftentimes people who have children older than your own can give you a heads-up on things to come, or can put you in touch with resources that they have used that would be beneficial to you as well.

Epilogue

The Story Continues

There is so much of Tré's life story that could not be contained in this book: subsequent surgeries, starting school, and other events in our family's life: losing a baby in the ninth month of pregnancy, travel, a new addition to the family in the form of my fifth and final child – my son Quinton. So much has happened, so many struggles, so many tears, so much laughter.

Tré has grown and flourished throughout it all. He has opened the door to his whole family meeting famous people! Meeting his favorite gospel artist Fred Hammond TWICE, posing with DC sports figures like Bryce Harper, Stephen Strassberg, and Ryan Zimmerman of the Washington Nationals; Fred Smoot, Santana Moss, and LaVar Arrington of the Washington Redskins have been but a few of the highlights of his life.

And he has accomplished greater and even more astonishing achievements – learning to walk, learning to talk, feeding orally and eventually discarding the feeding tube; learning to READ, learning to SING (constantly!), horseback riding, playing the piano and on and on and on. Suffice it to say my little baby who was not supposed to be able to move or do much of anything else has overcome just about every obstacle set before him. Even a more recent diagnosis of Autism isn't stopping him.

I continue to see my role as his cheerleader, his nurse, his educator, his therapist and his voice. And daily I am encouraged and determined to transform what was once adversity into advocacy not just for him, but for other parents and children who need someone to help them fight.

ABOUT THE AUTHOR

LaTanya S. Sothern has been an educator for over 20 years. She is a passionate supporter of special needs children and it is her mission to help them get services appropriate for their needs.

A native Washingtonian, she holds a Bachelor of Arts in Public Communication and Economics from The American University and a Master of Arts in Teaching with a concentration in Early Childhood Education from Howard University.

She is certified in Early Childhood Education, Special Education, and School Administration; achieved National Board Certification (Early Childhood Generalist); is the founder of the special-needs ministry at her church and is the President and C.E.O. of Sothern Education Solutions, LLC – offering special education consulting and advocacy.

She has been happily married to her husband Greg for 16 years. They have two sons, Thomas III (Tré) and Quinton, and reside in Prince George's County, Maryland.

For more information on this book,
education services, or booking visit:

www.sothernsolutions.com

Instagram: **@sothernsolution**
Twitter: **@sothernsolution**
Periscope: **@sothernsolution**
Facebook: **LaTanya S. Sothern,
Child Advocate and Author**

Made in the USA
Charleston, SC
19 October 2015